Prolific Author

The Step-by-Step Guide to Write More Words in Less Time and Finish Your Book Fast

WORKBOOK

Author Success Foundations Series Book 4

by
Christopher di Armani

ISBN-13: 978-1988938219

Editor: Nicolas Johnson

Published by

Botanie Valley Productions Inc.
PO Box 507
Lytton, BC V0K1Z0

https://BotanieValleyProductions.com
Sales@BotanieValleyProductions.com

Dedication

This book is dedicated to my sweet and loving wife Lynda.

Without her unwavering support of my need to write every day…

This book would not be possible.

Acknowledgments

Without the assistance of my editor, Nicolas Johnson, I can't imagine how this book would read. He tears my words apart from every conceivable angle, then offers thoughtful and constructive criticism on how best to fix the destruction at our feet.

I thank God for Nicolas Johnson and his talents, daily.

#EditorsMatter

Feedback Loop

I also wish to express my heartfelt gratitude to the following individuals who took time from their own busy lives to critique this manuscript. Their willingness to assist a total stranger humbles me.

Jendayi Harris (Facebook.com/JendayiH)
Kim Steadman (KimSteadman.com)
Sharilee Swaity (Facebook.com/Sharilee.Swaity)

Before You Begin

I recommend reading the book *Author Productivity Mindset* from front to back, twice, before completing this workbook. This will give you a greater understanding of the process and which areas to focus your efforts.

What Must You Do Every Day?

In the space below, write down every task you do each day, excluding your morning routine. This includes your daily commute, work, walking the dog, family time, and sports. Beside each item on your list, estimate how many hours you require for the activity.

_____

_____

_____

_____

_____

_____

_____

_____

_____

_____

_____

_____

_____

_____

_____

_____

_____

_____

_____

_____

_____

_____

_____

What Are Your Dreams?

Whatever your author dreams may be, write them down. Leave nothing out, no matter how far-fetched or impossible it seems. Remember, there is no right or wrong answers. These are your dreams, so embrace the process and be as diligent as possible when writing them all down. No dream is too silly or inconsequential. If it enters your mind, write it down.

What Are You Passionate About?

Think about your life, your past accomplishments, and make a list of everything you are passionate about. Rank your passions in order from most passionate to least. What does this list reveal to you? Write that down as well.

What Do You Value Most?

Write out a list of your daily activities. Beside each item on that list, write down how much time you spend on that activity. Include everything. How long you watch television, spend on Twitter, Facebook and other social media sites, hang out on your smart phone, coffee with friends, work, family time not spent glued to the idiot box, work, commuting to and from work. Create a comprehensive list of every activity you do each day.

Repeat this process for seven days using the Daily Activity Recording Sheets at the end of this workbook.

_____

_____

_____

_____

_____

_____

_____

_____

_____

_____

_____

_____

_____

_____

_____

_____

_____

_____

_____

_____

_____

_____

_____

_____

_____

_____

What Do You Want To Write?

In a few sentences, explain what your book is about and why it is important for you to write it.
Next, write down why you are the best person to write it, if not the only person who can write it.

_____

_____

_____

_____

_____

_____

_____

_____

_____

_____

_____

_____

_____

_____

_____

_____

_____

_____

_____

_____

_____

_____

_____

_____

_____

_____

_____

_____

Honest Self-Assessment

As discussed in the opening chapter of the book, every human being is driven by six core needs. Using one of the tests suggested in the book, which two core needs primarily drive you and your decision-making process?

Core Need #1: _____

Core Need #2: _____

Complete the following sentences.

I devote _____ minutes per day to writing.

To determine your words per hour, set a timer for 15 minutes and write until the timer expires. Repeat this test four times in one day. Your hourly word count is the combined total of your words written during these 15-minute sessions.

My hourly word count is _____ .

I write _____ hours per day.

Your daily word count equals your hourly word count multiplied by the number of hours you write per day.

My daily word count is: _____.

What is your deadline to complete your book? _____

How many days is that from today?   _____

Using the following formula, does the math work to achieve your goal?

TWR / WPD = N

N = Number of Days to Complete your Novel.

TWR = Total Words Required to Complete your Novel.

WPD = How Many Words You Write Per Day.

TWR _____ / WPD _____ = _____

Does the math work to achieve your deadline?

If not, what will you change in order to achieve your goal by your desired deadline?

_____

_____

_____

_____

_____

_____

_____

_____

_____

Daily Activity Recording Sheet

Date: _____

Activity	Time Spent

Daily Activity Recording Sheet

Date: _____

Activity	Time Spent

Daily Activity Recording Sheet

Date: _____

Activity	Time Spent

Daily Activity Recording Sheet

Date: _____

Activity	Time Spent

Daily Activity Recording Sheet

Date: _____

Activity	Time Spent

Daily Activity Recording Sheet

Date: _____

Activity	Time Spent

Daily Activity Recording Sheet

Date: _____

Activity	Time Spent

Daily Activity Recording Sheet

Date: _____

Activity	Time Spent

Writing Productivity Planner EXAMPLE

Here is a sample day for a writer with a full-time job, a spouse and two children. Use this as a guide when designing your day, with the ultimate goal of productive writing time every day.

6:00 am	Wake up, make coffee, morning meditation/reading
6:30	Work out for 30 minutes
7:00	Shower, brush teeth, get dressed for work
7:30	Go over schedule for the day
8:00	Daily morning commute to work
8:30	
9:00	Work
9:30	
10:00	
10:30	
11:00	
11:30	
12:00	Lunch Hour
12:30	
1:00 pm	Work
1:30	
2:00	
2:30	
3:00	
3:30	
4:00	
4:30	
5:00	Finished work, drive home
5:30	Evening Commute
6:00	Arrive home, dinner with family
6:30	
7:00	Family time
7:30	
8:00	Put kids to bed, spend quality time with spouse
8:30	
9:00	Write for one hour
10:00	Unwind, go to bed.

Writing Productivity Planner

Design your daily productivity plan below.

6:00 am _____

6:30 _____

7:00 _____

7:30 _____

8:00 _____

8:30 _____

9:00 _____

9:30 _____

10:00 _____

10:30_____

11:00 _____

11:30_____

12:00_____

12:30_____

1:00 pm _____

1:30 _____

2:00 _____

2:30 _____

3:00 _____

3:30 _____

4:00 _____

4:30 _____

5:00 _____

5:30 _____

6:00 _____

6:30 _____

7:00 _____

7:30 _____

8:00 _____

8:30 _____

9:00 _____

10:00 _____

11:00 _____

Writing Productivity Planner

Design your daily productivity plan below.

6:00 am _____

6:30 _____

7:00 _____

7:30 _____

8:00 _____

8:30 _____

9:00 _____

9:30 _____

10:00 _____

10:30 _____

11:00 _____

11:30 _____

12:00 _____

12:30 _____

1:00 pm _____

1:30 _____

2:00 _____

2:30 _____

3:00 _____

3:30 _____

4:00 _____

4:30 _____

5:00 _____

5:30 _____

6:00 _____

6:30 _____

7:00 _____

7:30 _____

8:00 _____

8:30 _____

9:00 _____

10:00 _____

11:00 _____

Writing Productivity Planner

Design your daily productivity plan below.

6:00 am _____

6:30 _____

7:00 _____

7:30 _____

8:00 _____

8:30 _____

9:00 _____

9:30 _____

10:00 _____

10:30 _____

11:00 _____

11:30 _____

12:00 _____

12:30 _____

1:00 pm _____

1:30 _____

2:00 _____

2:30 _____

3:00 _____

3:30 _____

4:00 _____

4:30 _____

5:00 _____

5:30 _____

6:00 _____

6:30 _____

7:00 _____

7:30 _____

8:00 _____

8:30 _____

9:00 _____

10:00 _____

11:00 _____

Writing Productivity Planner

Design your daily productivity plan below.

6:00 am _____

6:30 _____

7:00 _____

7:30 _____

8:00 _____

8:30 _____

9:00 _____

9:30 _____

10:00 _____

10:30 _____

11:00 _____

11:30 _____

12:00 _____

12:30 _____

1:00 pm _____

1:30 _____

2:00 _____

2:30 _____

3:00 _____

3:30 _____

4:00 _____

4:30 _____

5:00 _____

5:30 _____

6:00 _____

6:30 _____

7:00 _____

7:30 _____

8:00 _____

8:30 _____

9:00 _____

10:00 _____

11:00 _____

Writing Productivity Planner

Design your daily productivity plan below.

6:00 am _____

6:30 _____

7:00 _____

7:30 _____

8:00 _____

8:30 _____

9:00 _____

9:30 _____

10:00 _____

10:30 _____

11:00 _____

11:30 _____

12:00 _____

12:30 _____

1:00 pm _____

1:30 _____

2:00 _____

2:30 _____

3:00 _____

3:30 _____

4:00 _____

4:30 _____

5:00 _____

5:30 _____

6:00 _____

6:30 _____

7:00 _____

7:30 _____

8:00 _____

8:30 _____

9:00 _____

10:00 _____

11:00 _____

Writing Productivity Planner

Design your daily productivity plan below.

6:00 am _____

6:30 _____

7:00 _____

7:30 _____

8:00 _____

8:30 _____

9:00 _____

9:30 _____

10:00 _____

10:30 _____

11:00 _____

11:30 _____

12:00 _____

12:30 _____

1:00 pm _____

1:30 _____

2:00 _____

2:30 _____

3:00 _____

3:30 _____

4:00 _____

4:30 _____

5:00 _____

5:30 _____

6:00 _____

6:30 _____

7:00 _____

7:30 _____

8:00 _____

8:30 _____

9:00 _____

10:00 _____

11:00 _____

Writing Productivity Planner

Design your daily productivity plan below.

6:00 am _____

6:30 _____

7:00 _____

7:30 _____

8:00 _____

8:30 _____

9:00 _____

9:30 _____

10:00 _____

10:30 _____

11:00 _____

11:30 _____

12:00 _____

12:30 _____

1:00 pm _____

1:30 _____

2:00 _____

2:30 _____

3:00 _____

3:30 _____

4:00 _____

4:30 _____

5:00 _____

5:30 _____

6:00 _____

6:30 _____

7:00 _____

7:30 _____

8:00 _____

8:30 _____

9:00 _____

10:00 _____

11:00 _____

Writing Productivity Planner

Design your daily productivity plan below.

6:00 am _____

6:30 _____

7:00 _____

7:30 _____

8:00 _____

8:30 _____

9:00 _____

9:30 _____

10:00 _____

10:30 _____

11:00 _____

11:30 _____

12:00 _____

12:30 _____

1:00 pm _____

1:30 _____

2:00 _____

2:30 _____

3:00 _____

3:30 _____

4:00 _____

4:30 _____

5:00 _____

5:30 _____

6:00 _____

6:30 _____

7:00 _____

7:30 _____

8:00 _____

8:30 _____

9:00 _____

10:00 _____

11:00 _____

Congratulations!

You did it! You created your daily writing routine.

Time to apply self-discipline to achieve your goals. For me, this is a daily battle. At my core, I'm lazy. I love writing but I want the easy road to publication. I don't want to do the hard work required.

A daily routine is B-O-R-I-N-G.

It's also the simplest, fastest and most effective way to finish my book.

I didn't build this system because I was bored one day. I built it because I knew, through my own pain, suffering and failure, I needed to change my writing process if I wanted to finish my book.

I am far happier when I follow the structure of my daily routine. I write more words, better words, faster than any other time in my life. Seven books and four workbooks published in three months is a pretty incredible accomplishment, and one I could never achieve without my daily routine and personal writing productivity system.

My fervent prayer is for you to take the same leap of faith I did and join me on a pilgrimage down Publication Highway. This is an amazing journey and one you do not want to miss!

Building a routine to support your writing life is the best thing you can do for your creative self. I would love to hear what you felt as you went through this experience.

https://ChristopherDiArmani.net/contact/

Sincerely,

Christopher

Christopher di Armani
Author Success Foundations

Next Steps

Join me on the incredible journey down Publication Highway and learn the secret of Getting to Done.

Done is Better Than Perfect - Seven Keys to Finish Writing Your Book Fast, the fifth book in the Author Success Foundations series, explains how perfectionism kills dreams and why finishing is always better than failure.

The fundamental truths of writing:

1. Your book will never be perfect.

2. You cannot publish what you do not complete.

3. Done is better than perfect. Always.

Accept these truths and move on.

Available from your favorite online book retailers today.

For more information, visit:

https://ChristopherDiArmani.net/design-your-morning-routine

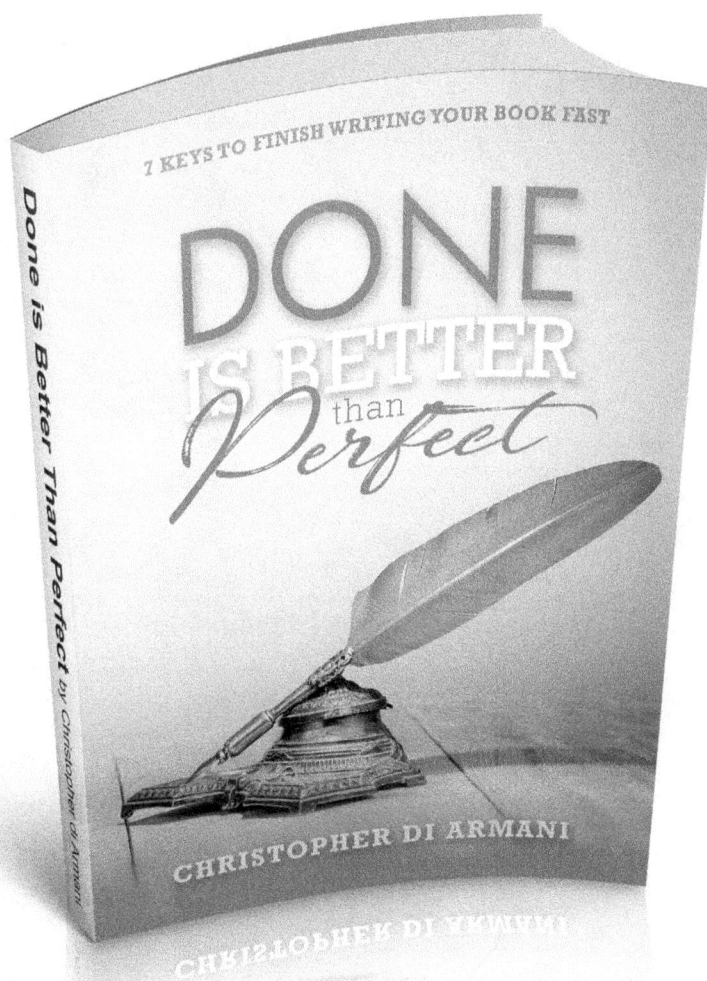